A SPIRIT DAUGHTER WORKBOOK

WRITTEN BY
JILL WINTERSTEEN

FOR THE FULL MOON

SUNDAY, OCTOBER 9TH, 2022
1:54PM PT

02

WHY THE FULL MOON

The Full Moon is a time of opposition, but also a time of significant growth. On a Full Moon, the Sun and Moon stand directly opposite one another in our sky. They face each other head-on to bring out the full spectrum of energies held by both cosmic bodies. Their opposition illuminates the seen and unseen, the known and unknown, the shadow and the light. Under this full view, we can feel into the entire array of our own consciousness. We can bring energies to the surface of the mind so we may work with them, shift them, and ultimately transform ourselves. Each Full Moon brings us opportunities, but with these gifts come challenges—ones we must accept and overcome to become our best self.

THE FEMININE AND THE MASCULINE
Each of us is a delicate balance of feminine and masculine energy. Regardless of gender, these energies exist in all of us to varying degrees. The Sun represents our masculine energy—our doing side. This is the part of us that wants to take action with logic and practicality. Solar energy can feel forceful when imbalanced, as it tries to take over and control situations. In balance, it motivates and inspires us to intelligently use our will to overcome adversities.

The Moon represents our feminine energy. This is our being or receiving side—the part of us that wants to use intuition to feel into our next steps. Our feminine energy reminds us to stay soft, fluid, and capable of change as things shift around us. Lunar energy can feel passive when imbalanced, leaving life up to others as it waits for the next step. In balance, it allows us to receive answers effortlessly as our inner knowledge guides the way through life's challenges.

On the Full Moon, masculine and feminine confront each other in the sky, providing the opportunity to reconcile these polarities within us. We can fully see where imbalances lie in both of these vibrations and adjust them as necessary, so they work together—not against one another. On any Full Moon, ask yourself where in your life you might be trying too hard to force things by overthinking or relying too heavily on logic. Likewise, where can you soften and open yourself up to receiving answers through feeling and intuition?

ASTROLOGICAL INFLUENCES
The Sun and Moon are positioned in opposing zodiac signs each Full Moon, bringing these astrological vibrations into our energetic field. Opposing zodiac signs form an axis of energy consisting of extreme sides, which directly oppose one another then meet in the middle to find some common ground. The extreme ends of this spectrum hold the signs' shadow side, where imbalances often occur. The middle, or balance point, is where both signs' higher vibratory energies merge to form a frequency composed of the two astrological energies, more magnificent than each sign alone.

On a Full Moon, we have the opportunity to work with both zodiac signs involved. We can clearly see where we may be aligned with the extreme sides of the sign. Once we understand how we embrace each sign's shadow side, we can release it and transform it. This revelation takes courage and the willingness on our part to see ourselves from every angle. If we take on the challenge of viewing and accepting our shadows, we have a chance to bring balance to the part of ourselves illuminated by the Full Moon. We have the opportunity to form the balance point between each zodiac sign involved on this day and raise our very vibration to a new level. It takes work, though, and that is the purpose of this workbook: to help you harness the opportunity of each Full Moon to make big shifts in your energy as you move away from your shadows and step into the power of your full light.

ARIES FULL MOON

In the midst of a peaceful Libra Season, we are met by the Aries Full Moon. Ruled by Fire, Aries brings us the opportunity to burn away anything blocking our path forward. This Full Moon is a time to align with your inner power and feel your courage to overcome any obstacle. It's also a time to align with your passions. Aries guides us on the mission to find our soul's purpose. Finding this path takes commitment, motivation, and fearlessness. Our life path is not always an easy journey. This Full Moon is here to help you walk a little farther on it with more confidence than you've ever felt before.

The first step in understanding this Full Moon is to know that it can bring up feelings of restlessness, impatience, and frustration. Aries quickly points out where you are not aligning with your life's purpose. This energy can feel intense and cause self-doubt in your decisions. It is here to inspire you to break through anything holding you back from the reason you were born in this lifetime. If you are not currently aligned with your soul or on a path to finding its mission, this Full Moon can feel very challenging. It may even cause energetic breakdowns in your system, including internal tantrums, many tears, and even bursts of anger toward those around you. If you find yourself in any of these vibrations, take a moment to settle your energy. Align with your breath and move your body. Exercise is one of the best things you can do for yourself on an Aries Full Moon. Break a sweat, move your energy, and notice where you are attacking yourself or others.

There is a fine line in the brain between anger and motivation. If you find yourself feeling angry or frustrated this Full Moon, ask yourself what you can do with the energy. This Moon can be a powerful time to break through self-imposed limitations

ARIES FULL MOON

that are causing stagnation in your life. When our energy stagnates or does not move forward, we tend to feel restless and impatient. We also tend to feel these things when we are not making the choices needed to align with our soul's journey. We may not know what choices need to be made, which can also be frustrating. Instead of getting lost in a sea of anger on this Full Moon, know you can direct this internal fire. Use it to break through your fears, confusion, doubt, or misdirection. Anger can be powerful, and it can help you take action where you need to in your life. It's all a matter of directing it.

It's also important to note that when anger comes up, it can be a signal that your boundaries are being, or have been, infringed upon. When we feel that our energy is being invaded or that we are not being seen or respected, we become angry. This is a natural part of being human and a clue that you need to state your needs more firmly. This does not mean stating them more aggressively or with force, but simply with firmness and power. It can be challenging to ask for what you need, especially from the people closest to you.

This Aries Full Moon, though, is the time to look at how the boundaries in your relationships may be weak. If anger often arises in your relationships, ask yourself if there are things you need to say that you may be avoiding. Ask yourself why you are avoiding them. Then think of how you can calmly and constructively state your needs in a manner that reinforces your boundaries and dissipates your frustration. This may not be the exact time to have a needed conversation, but it is still a good time to think about which words need to be said.

This is also a Moon of forgiveness. Every Full Moon brings us an opportunity to forgive ourselves and others. With Aries theming this Full Moon, it's an important time to look at how you may be holding anger toward yourself or another. Then ask yourself if you are ready to forgive. We do not forgive other people for them. We forgive them for ourselves. Staying angry takes up much energy. Holding resentment toward somebody consumes our valuable resources. It also prevents us from raising our vibration to frequencies of love and compassion. It is also very difficult to exist in higher frequencies if we are angry at either ourselves or someone else.

It's important to know that when you forgive someone, it does not mean you are condoning or approving of their behavior. It simply means that you are releasing the energy that attaches you to them. You are severing the energetic cord between yourself and a person or situation. Through this release, you take back your energy and your power. When you remain angry at someone, you give them a bit of your power because you are holding space in your energetic field for them. Remaining angry at someone means you need to think about them. It means they are taking up some of your mental space and consuming your energy.

On this Full Moon, ask yourself if you need to forgive anyone. Also, ask if you need to forgive yourself. Staying angry with yourself is energetically draining and can prohibit you from moving forward on your path. You may even be self-sabotaging out of anger or frustration. It can be very challenging to forgive yourself. Remember that you are only human and allowed to make mistakes. Nothing positive can come out of you being at war with yourself. Allow this Full Moon to open your heart and help you enter a compassionate frequency. Have compassion for yourself and others. Then, from a place of compassion and courage, forgive yourself and anyone else. Not because they necessarily deserve it, but because you do.

ARIES MOON X LIBRA SUN

While the Moon lands in Aries, the Sun remains in Libra, allowing us to work with both of these vibrations in our energetic bodies. On Full Moons, the Sun opposes the Moon, revealing a spectrum of energies, both high and low. We have the opportunity to release any lower frequencies we may be aligning with and transform them into higher ones. It starts, though, by being aware of what frequencies are available to us to work on during a Full Moon, then becoming aware of which ones we are aligning with in our behaviors, thoughts, and emotions.

Aries and Libra sit opposite each other in the sky and on the zodiac wheel. Aries is home to the First House of the self and ruled by Mars, while Libra is home to the Seventh House of relationships and ruled by Venus. On the surface, these two energies are as different as can be. When we look a little closer, they can teach us valuable lessons about staying aligned with our soul's journey while sharing the experience of living it with another.

Aries reminds us this Full Moon that we have a purpose in this life, and when we find it, we feel content. Libra encourages us to feel at peace no matter the situation, which is more easily achieved when aligned with our soul's path. Furthermore, we have a better chance of forming healthy relationships and partnerships when we have a purpose and feel fulfilled on our own. This Full Moon reminds us that we are already whole. People in our lives do not complete us. Instead, they make life that much sweeter. The real relationship to observe during this season is the one with yourself.

Aries and Libra both carry the warrior spirit. Aries is more aggressive, depicting the typical warrior ready to fight through adversity to rise to the next level. Libra is more of a peaceful warrior, who battles only when balance has been disturbed. Aries gives us the energy to conquer some of our toughest demons, while Libra helps us right the wrongs done to us or those we've done to others. Aries also fights with fire and force, while Libra uses air composed of words and balanced communications. Aries, though, is direct and often unstoppable. When we invoke the energy of Aries, change happens. We send the message, and there is no misinterpreting the meaning. Libra, on the other hand, is softer and often can be swayed to another side. Libra tends to see all sides equally, which can be beneficial. But it can also make this energy less effective in creating change quickly. The vibration of Libra asks that we first understand the whole issue from all sides before making a decision. This understanding can take time and may lose momentum.

When we look at Aries's higher vibrations, we see courage, determination, stamina and drive. This energy helps us make decisions quickly and confidently. It also helps us dissolve obstacles with determination and sheer willpower. This is the energy of the Ram, ready to act when needed and not allowing anything to stop it. We need this energy in our lives when we are facing adversities, starting something new, or choosing to focus on ourselves. It allows us to make challenging choices that demand we put ourselves first. It also helps us understand when being selfish can be beneficial for our evolution and the overall vibration of the world. Aries teaches us that when we put ourselves and our missions first, everyone benefits. Our path may require us to choose it over and over again. Aries gives us the energy needed to choose our soul's journey even when it's not the easy one.

Aries in its low, or shadow, frequencies does become negatively selfish. When we align with this side, we forget that we live in a world full of other people. We lose our ability to compromise or make choices for the sake of peace. We stand our ground even when it's not worth the battle. We may even start battles just for the sake of proving a point with no real intention behind the energy. Aries's lower frequencies cause us to make ourselves the only priority. It also causes us to focus on only our perspective, giving us a one-sided vision, as we forget to see things from another's point of view.

ARIES MOON X LIBRA SUN

Selfishness is a fine line. We need enough of it to stay true to our journey and not give into other people's demands when they challenge our commitment to ourselves. Too much selfishness, though, causes us to live a life of solitude or unbalanced relationships. When we take too much energy, it doesn't feel good. We intuitively know when relationships are unbalanced. We may not know how to correct it, but we know that something if off. This feeling of imbalance causes frustration and anger— other low sides of Aries. As you work with the Full Moon, ask yourself where you may have crossed the line of selfishness. Where do you need to be more selfish for the sake of your soul? And where do you need to be less selfish for the sake of your partnerships? Align with the Full Moon to shift these energies. Make yourself a priority, but also know where and how you can compromise. There are things in this life that are non-negotiable, and there are things that we can loosen our grip on. Decide on this Full Moon what you are willing to fight for, what you are willing to stand your ground on, and what you are willing to negotiate over for another person's happiness. Helping others be happy in turn makes us happy in our hearts and can sometimes be more important than proving a point.

This Full Moon also helps us shed the lower vibrations of Libra, which can work against the search for our purpose. The low, or shadow, side of the scales is passive-aggressiveness and indecision. When we align with this side, we vacillate between choices and often become frustrated. We cannot decide on a path, and we question our instinctual knowledge. We lose trust in ourselves and can run around in circles, never finding our way. Being indecisive is another way we battle with ourselves, and this war can spill onto others. This constant wavering can pressure our relationships as we look to others for answers, not understanding that we already hold the answers we seek. We also tend to lean on others' support instead of our own inner strength to help us on our journeys. This behavior can lead to codependency and a sense of losing ourselves in another.

If you find yourself aligning with the lower vibrations of Libra, it's best to spend some time in meditation, learning to trust yourself without outside influence. Ask yourself some questions and notice the first answers that appear. Do not overanalyze them, but allow them to come from your intuition. Feel your gut response and go with it. Take action and know that if things don't go the way you want them to, there will always be a lesson to learn and room to grow. Give yourself the grace to make missteps on your path. This allowance will encourage you to pick a road and walk it.

As we step away from the lower vibrations of Aries and Libra, we allow ourselves to align with our soul's purpose. We understand that when we feel content and fulfilled, everyone in our life benefits. We can balance the priority and responsibility to ourselves with our responsibilities to others. We know when to compromise, when to fight for what we love, and how to make peace with our soul's journey. This Full Moon has the power to teach us about our soul's purpose and how to pursue it while living in the world with other people—each of whom has their own soul's purpose. When we integrate the higher vibrations of Libra and Aries, we know how to support both ourselves and others. We also know when to ask for support and even choose partners who help evolve us to the next level of our personal journey.

This Moon can help you understand your journey more deeply and in turn help you develop more fulfilling relationships. Ideally, you want partners who also understand how to balance their life's mission with yours so that each person feels fulfilled and without resentment. Align with this Full Moon to create a life full of purpose, passion, and enjoyment. Then learn how to make it a priority while still sharing the experience and joy of life with others.

ASPECTS

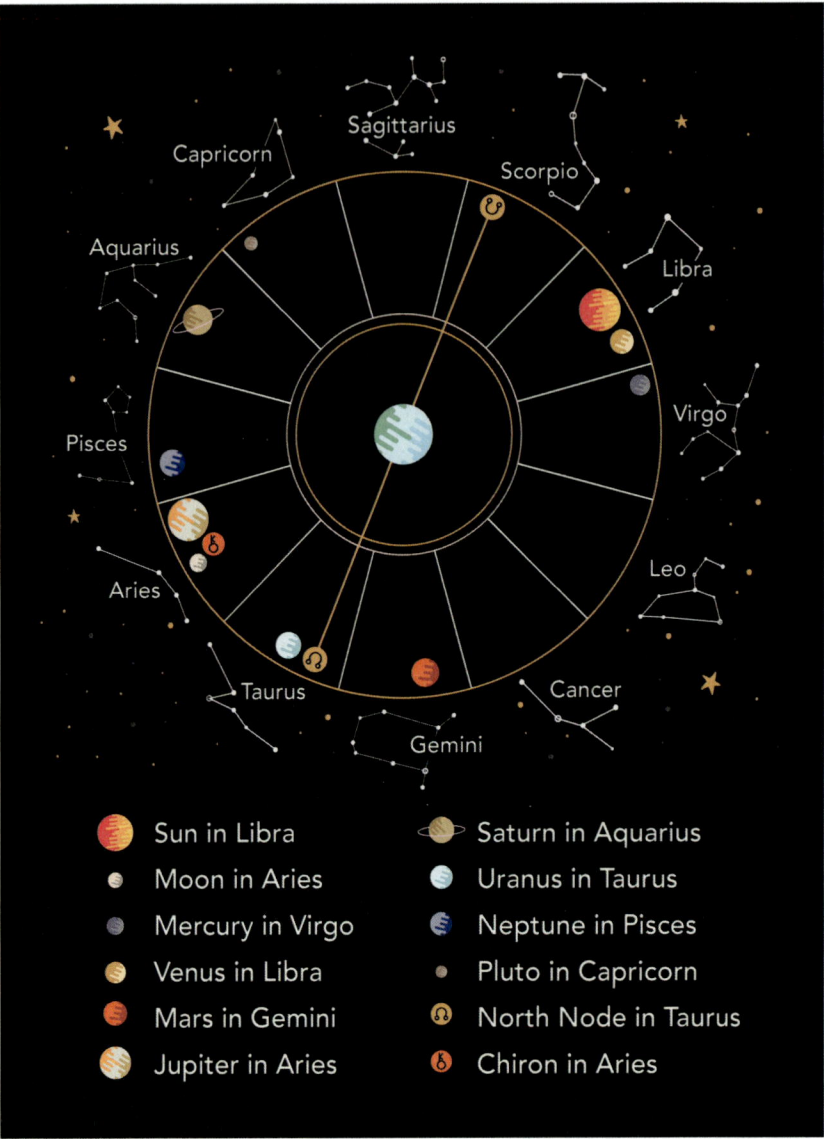

Sun in Libra

Moon in Aries

Mercury in Virgo

Venus in Libra

Mars in Gemini

Jupiter in Aries

Saturn in Aquarius

Uranus in Taurus

Neptune in Pisces

Pluto in Capricorn

North Node in Taurus

Chiron in Aries

The Moon and Sun do not exist in the sky alone. They are surrounded by other planets, each of which has an energy and vibration. These other planets influence the energy of the Full Moon. They give us some additional aspects to work with in our emotional and energetic bodies.

This Full Moon carries a lot of Air energy. The planetary ruler of Aries, Mars, is positioned in Gemini, while the Sun is in Libra. Saturn also lands in Aquarius, creating a Grand Air Trine between these three cosmic bodies. If you could map them out in the sky, they would form a giant triangle, amplifying the Air element and its corresponding vibrations. Air stirs our mental realm. It quickens our thoughts and can make us feel ungrounded. It also helps us exchange ideas quickly. Air wants us to connect with others. It reminds us that we share much in common with those around us. After all, we all breathe the same air.

Mixed with the Fire of Aries, Air can become dangerous if we don't take the time to connect with our body and breath. Fire is a mix of Air and Earth. Air pulls Fire upward and expands it, while Earth anchors it and gives it stability. Too much Air can cause Fire to become uncontrollable, while too little Air can make it ineffective. On this Full Moon, feel what helps your fire burn brightly and feel what grounds it. Uncontrolled fire can look like untamed anger, manic behavior that leads to burnout, or communication that overwhelms others. Notice if any of these energies come up for you today or any day, and commit to practices that help you ground yourself.

Be aware that this Full Moon is surrounded by Air and may cause you to feel even more restless or impatient than normal. It may cause you to overtalk, overshare, or give in to bursts of frustration. If you feel like you're having an internal tantrum this Full Moon, take a step back from the situation and give yourself time to process the events. Ask yourself what is pulling on your internal fire. Also, ask yourself how you are grounding this fire so that it doesn't get out of control and burn either yourself or others.

Once you learn how to tame your internal fire, it becomes very powerful. The element of Air present during this Full Moon gives you the opportunity to connect different ideas very effectively. It also allows you to release energy quickly. This Full Moon can help you let go, forgive, and remove obstacles in your path with ease. Feel the Air element helping you swiftly remove things from your life, call in new energies, and connect the dots.

The Moon also involves the energy of Venus. The Sun is conjunct Venus in Libra, while the Moon in Aries opposes it. Venus is the planet of love. It teaches us how we love and what we need to feel loved. As it meets the Sun in Libra, Venus draws attention to our relationships. It helps us feel the ones that feed our hearts and the ones that distract from it. As Venus opposes the Full Moon, it sheds light on choices we make for love that may sacrifice the soul's mission.

The involvement of Venus this Full Moon asks you to become aware of what choices you make out of love for yourself and what choices you make out of love for others. There is also the component of looking at what choices you make to feel loved by others. It's often these decisions and behaviors that draw us away from our truth. When we seek love from another, we can fall prey to changing our behavior to fit their needs or desires. Notice this Full Moon if you are sacrificing any of your own truths and passions to gain love from another. The right people in your life will love you for your passions and your soul. They will appreciate you just the way you are and will support decisions you need to make to align with your life's purpose. They will light your fire instead of draining it.

As you work with the influence of Venus on this Full Moon, feel your heart. Let it lead you to your true desires, and let it help you put yourself first. Making yourself a priority isn't selfish. It's necessary to align with your life's path. And when you're aligned with your life's path, everyone benefits.

MARS PLACEMENTS

Just as we all have a Sun and a Moon sign, we also have a Mars sign, the place Mars was positioned when we were born. In your natal chart, Mars shows where your true passions lie, where your fire burns for more, and where, or how, you may become hot-tempered. It can also tell you what motivates you the most and what can help you transition out of stagnation and into action.

Mars is the ruling planet of Aries. On the Full Moon in Aries, Mars is also activated and plays a role in how you will experience this Full Moon. By knowing your Mars placement, you can pay attention to the part of your personality ruled by Mars. These areas are amplified on the Aries Full Moon, and you can understand them more deeply as the Moon highlights them. In the following pages, you can find a description of the energy Mars brings to your chart and personality determined by its placement in the sky when you were born. You can look up your chart at astro-charts.com.

MARS PLACEMENTS

MARS IN ARIES

Mars is at home in your chart. Mars in Aries gives you drive, ambition, and fearlessness. That's not to say you don't get scared from time to time, but you never allow fear to run your life. Instead, you use fear as a tool to develop courage. You head straight into situations that would panic most people. You do not see them as a reason to run but as an opportunity to strengthen your enduring spirit. You see stress as an experience that is motivating and illuminating. You are here to learn through challenging life circumstances and welcome them like a confident warrior entering battle, knowing you will always prevail. Feel this strength and power in your spirit awaken this Full Moon. Ask yourself: "How do I want to channel this fire to make the most out of my life?"

MARS IN TAURUS

Mars in Taurus gives you tenacity, patience, and strong willpower. You are slow to fight for anything, but when you do, you put all of your energy into it. You are quite a force, and when you desire something, the world better watch out. Most days, though, you fight for serenity. You desire quiet mornings, time in the solace of nature, and days spent in comfortable surroundings. When you are at peace with yourself, it seems the world is less chaotic. When this peace is disturbed, though, you can become impatient, hot-tempered, and restless. You may find that life hands you many situations that challenge your inner harmony and ask you to develop tools that restore your calmness. Developing practices may not always be easy, but once you do, you commit your full energy to them. You are able to climb any mountain and overcome any obstacle once you feel at home within yourself. Feel this strength of the Full Moon. Ask yourself: "What is so important that I am willing to disturb my peace, and how will I then return to it?"

MARS IN GEMINI

Mars in Gemini gives you a keen intelligence, a thirst for knowledge, and a powerful voice. You are here to learn, question, and form opinions. You are also here to communicate your knowledge while constantly learning more. You are open to many experiences and see every situation, person, or energy as your teacher. If you feel afraid of something new, you confront that fear and do not let it block you from a chance to evolve. You also have the ability to battle with words and can use them as weapons. Be kind to those around you—they may not have the ability to respond as quickly as you can in an argument. Always have compassion when speaking about your needs or when in a debate. Be a heart-centered warrior and know that speaking with your heart is the greatest lesson you'll ever learn. On this Full Moon, be aware of your words and their power. Ask yourself: "How am I ready to use my voice to put more positive energy into the world even if I am met with opposition?"

MARS IN CANCER

Mars in Cancer gives you a warrior spirit when facing your emotions, or anyone else's. You do not shy away from painful topics, buckets of tears, or heartfelt speeches. You approach all feelings with acceptance and bravery. You innately understand that it takes courage to feel. You are here to hold space for your feelings and find their power. Emotions are the doorway to your intuition. When you face them with an open heart, they give you knowledge needed for your life's path. The more you can open up to your feelings, the more you understand your purpose this lifetime and how to align with your soul. It's important that you make time to listen to yourself and set boundaries that protect your inner space. On this Full Moon, feel your heart. Ask yourself: "Is there anyone I need to forgive so I may feel more deeply?"

MARS PLACEMENTS

MARS IN LEO

Mars in Leo gives you confidence and the courage to speak your heart. You are here to face vulnerability and overcome any fears you have around being seen. You are here to love life and let other people see you do it. You are also here to lead. You have a natural charisma that takes over the energy of any room. You light up a space, and all eyes turn to you. This may have felt uncomfortable in your younger years, but as you grow older, you become more accustomed to the spotlight. Instead of fearing it, you see it as an opportunity to form a platform. From here, you can do anything once you allow yourself to be seen. Always allow yourself to be motivated by love and your heart rather than fear. Your heart is your greatest tool. Let it lead you forward on your path. On this Full Moon, overcome any fear of the spotlight and let yourself be seen. Ask yourself: "Why am I hiding my true talents when they could change the world?"

MARS IN VIRGO

Mars in Virgo gives you a strong will to find your gift and work on it. You are here to give a piece of yourself to the world and stop at nothing until you find this offering. You will work relentlessly on yourself until you feel good enough and strong enough to be of service. You must be wary of perfectionism or obsessing over small details. Face your fears of imperfection with love and compassion for yourself. It is important to realize that you have a strong mission to help the world. You can overcome any obstacle when sharing your talents with the world. Feel your strength this Full Moon and find a mentor who can help you recognize your talent. Ask yourself: "What could I do if I allowed myself?"

MARS IN LIBRA

Mars in Libra loses a bit of its fire. The peaceful vibrations of Libra tame the warrior spirit of Mars. But the red planet is still very powerful once this energy finds its path. Mars in Libra inspires you to fight for what and how you love. However, you must be careful that it doesn't cause you to create unnecessary conflict with your partners. Instead, this energy can inspire you to fight for unions that raise the vibration of both parties. It also encourages you to find partners who can support your life path and are willing to help you fight for the life you deserve. This energy can help you cultivate partnerships that feel supportive and enlightening. If a partnership begins to drain too much energy, this placement can motivate you to make the changes needed to balance the union, or walk away. Feel this energy activated in you on this Full Moon. Harness it to make needed decisions about your partners and your life path. Ask yourself: "What partnerships are worth fighting for and which ones need a peaceful break?"

MARS IN SCORPIO

Mars in Scorpio is a powerful placement. As one of Scorpio's rulers, Mars thrives in this sign. This energy encourages you to face your shadows head-on. You do not run from your demons, but rather sit down and have tea with them. Fear fuels you and teaches you how to master your internal space. You eagerly charge into any situation that feels uncomfortable or foreign. You know these are the experiences that help you evolve the most. You seek out the mystery of life. Anything that frightens most people excites you. Feel your inner flame ignited this Full Moon. Get even more curious about exploring the depths of your soul. Face any fear holding you back and dissolve it with innate power. Ask yourself: "What am I ready to face that once blocked me but that now I will use for fuel?"

MARS PLACEMENTS

MARS IN SAGITTARIUS
Mars in Sagittarius gives you the strength and determination to open your mind. You have a natural thirst for knowledge that is sometimes satisfied by travel. What you really desire are new experiences that come in many forms to ignite your passion. You may feel stagnant, energetically drained, or even frustrated if you do not incorporate new vibrations into your life regularly. Channel your motivation into traveling the globe and absorbing as much as you can from people different from you. Allow your travels to help you find your soul, and know that your life's mission may be found on the road. Feel your inner desire to seek novelty on this Full Moon. Let it encourage you to break out of the mold you've been in and experience something you haven't before. Ask yourself: "What new experience is calling me?"

MARS IN CAPRICORN
Mars in Capricorn gives you the stamina to climb the tallest mountains and conquer any challenge in your way. You tend to direct your fire toward your work. You are fiercely dedicated to your life's mission and allow nothing to stop you from pursuing it. You must remember to take breaks to restore your fire, or you burn out your resources. If you start to feel resentful or frustrated by your work, take a break. Recharge your battery even if rest feels like a waste of time. Rest can be productive, especially when you need it. Once you feel restored, your focus will return and you will be even more unstoppable than before. Feel this Full Moon strengthen your resolve to find work that matters in your life. Align with your passions and make needed changes in your course. Ask yourself: "What is worth my powerful attention and energy?"

MARS IN AQUARIUS
Mars in Aquarius gives you the strength to fight for who you are in this life. You fiercely defend your freedom and your voice. You take firm stands on many issues and have the ability to lead the collective to new heights. You must be careful not to become frustrated with people who do not understand your visions. Not everyone will, and that's ok. Do not waste your breath on people who are determined to misunderstand you. Instead, use your energy to convey messages to people willing to open their perspectives to the future. Fight for what you believe and the future you see, but not so much that it drains your energy or makes you lose your love for life. Always remember to cultivate compassion for yourself and others, especially if you feel completely misunderstood. Feel your strength to speak your mind this Full Moon. Ask yourself: "What am I ready to say even if I am misunderstood?"

MARS IN PISCES
Mars in Pisces brings the strength to face spiritual battles required for soul evolution. This placement encourages you to dive deep into practices that open your mind, expand your consciousness, and ask you to accept different realities. It also creates a great passion within you for finding enlightenment and trying every tool that could get you there. You do not fear experimenting with your conscious or subconscious mind, but rather look forward to any opportunity that teaches you something new about yourself. On this Full Moon, feel your passion for evolving your consciousness take priority in your life. Feel motivated to take up new spiritual endeavors and paths. Ask yourself: "What forms of spirituality can lead me to my soul's path?"

ARIES LUNAR FLOW

SUN SALUTATION A // 3 ROUNDS

Stand at the top of your mat. Inhale, stretch your arms overhead > Exhale, fold forward > Inhale, lengthen out your back > Exhale, step back to Plank Pose and lower > Inhale, reach your chest up for Cobra Pose, legs on the ground > Exhale, Downward Dog Pose. Stay here for 5 breaths and feel your entire body expand. On exhale, step to the top of your mat > Inhale, lengthen through your spine > Exhale, fold forward > Inhale, come all the way up to standing, reaching arms overhead > Exhale, hands to your heart. Pause for a moment and feel yourself centered throughout your body.

SUN SALUTATION B // 3 ROUNDS

Stand at the top of your mat. Inhale, stretch your arms overhead, and bend your knees into Chair Pose > Exhale, fold forward > Inhale, lengthen out your back > Exhale, step into Plank Pose and lower half way to Chatarunga (elbows into ribs) > Inhale, reach your chest up for Upward-Facing Dog, with everything off the ground except your hands and feet > Exhale, Downward Dog Pose > Inhale, step left foot forward to Warrior 1, with your back foot flat at a 45-degree angle. Bend into your front knee and lift your arms to the sky, taking 5 breaths here > Exhale, release into Plank > lower to Chatarunga > Inhale into Upward-Facing Dog > Exhale, Downward Facing Dog. Repeat on right side, then remain in Downward Dog for 5 breaths > Exhale, step to the top of your mat > Inhale, lengthen through your spine > Exhale, fold forward > Inhale, Chair Pose > Exhale, hands to heart, breathe at the top of your mat as you feel your energy circulating throughout your body.

WARRIOR 2 > EXTENDED WARRIOR >
TRIANGLE POSE

Step your feet three to four feet wide on your mat facing the side. Turn your left foot toward the back of the mat and angle your back foot to 45 degrees. Bend in your front knee and reach your arms out to either side. Breathe here for 5 breaths and feel your hips open. After 5 breaths, place your left forearm to your left thigh and extend your right arm in line with your ear. Take 5 more breaths here. Begin to feel the strength of your legs supporting you, reminding you of your warrior spirit. During inhale, come back up to Warrior 2, straighten your front leg, and hinge forward into Triangle Pose. Place your left hand on the ground on the outside of your left foot or on your shin, and rotate your torso to the right. Stretch and reach upward through your right arm, feeling one long line of energy from fingertip to fingertip. After 5 breaths, come back upright and return your feet to parallel. Feel the strength of your body, which is ready to take on any challenge. Repeat on your right side.

Visit spiritdaughter.com/collections/zodiac-yoga to flow with our Aries Zodiac Yoga video.

ARIES LUNAR FLOW

STANDING APANASANA > WARRIOR 3 > LUNGE POSE

Step back to the top of your mat. Feel both feet on the ground as you steady your gaze. Shift your weight into your left foot. Pick your right foot off the ground, bending your knee and hugging it into the chest for standing Apanasana. Take 5 breaths here as you reach up through your chest and press down through your left foot. Without placing your foot down, release your knee and stretch your right leg back behind you, tilting your torso forward parallel to the ground for Warrior 3. You may press your hands together at heart center or reach your arms forward for the full pose. Take 5 breaths here, then place your left foot on the ground behind you for Lunge Pose. Tilt your pelvis down to the ground and stretch your arms up to the sky. Press firmly though your back leg as you bend to a 90-degree angle in your front leg. Take 5 breaths here, then step back to the top of your mat and repeat on the other side.

SIDE PLANK

From the top of your mat, inhale as you reach your arms overhead. Exhale, fold forward. Inhale, lengthen out your back. Exhale, step back into a Plank Pose. Hold as you shift your weight to your left hand. Pivot both feet to the left, stacking your right foot over your left (toes pointing to the right side of your mat). Rotate your chest to the right as you reach your right arm to the ceiling. Draw your lower belly in, directing your tailbone to your heels. Expand through your chest as you draw your shoulders down your back. Take 5 breaths here, feeling the heat and strength building in your core. After 5 breaths, come back to Plank Pose. Rest if you need to, then switch sides. Afterward, press back into Downward Dog and take 5 deep breaths. On exhale, step your feet to the top of your mat. Inhale, lengthen out your back. Exhale, fold forward. Inhale, come up to standing while reaching your arms overhead. Exhale, hands to heart center.

SQUAT POSE WITH BREATH OF FIRE

Separate your feet hips width apart, and turn your toes out to 45 degrees. Sit down into a squat; if needed, place a rolled-up towel underneath your heels. Bring your hands to your heart and press your elbows into your legs, opening your hips. Lengthen through your spine and take a deep inhale. During exhale, make short, sharp exhales through your nose, snapping your belly back to your spine. Pump your belly for 20 rounds, focusing only on the exhale. Once completed, take another deep inhale and hold the breath for 10 seconds, then exhale completely.

SAVASANA

Release onto the floor, lying with your palms up and eyes closed. Feel your body alive with fresh energy circulating freely through your body.

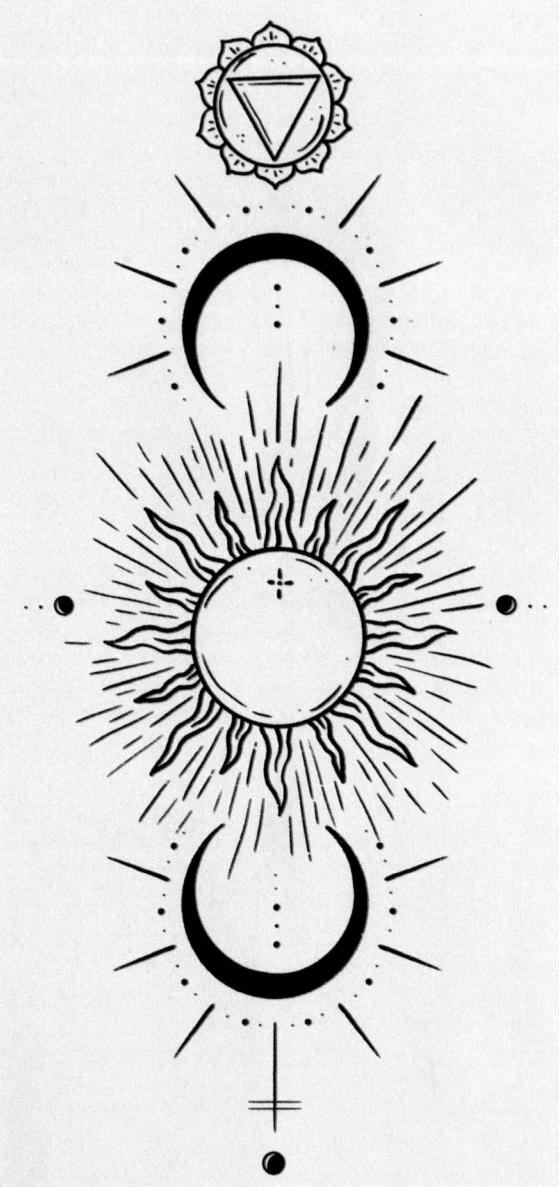

ARIES MEDITATION

Breath of Fire is a rhythmic breath focused on the exhale. It helps move the energy of the body, breaking up any stagnation. It also helps create motivation by fanning the internal flames while ensuring they don't burn out. To prepare for this breathwork, practice the exhale. Take a short, sharp exhale out of your nose as if you were trying to blow out a candle. You will feel your belly pulling back as you exhale, helping force the air out. This is the exhale you will use for Breath of Fire.

Come to a comfortable seated position with your spine upright. Lift up through the crown of your head, relaxing your shoulders. Close your eyes. Inhale about two-thirds of your lung capacity, then take 20 short, sharp exhales as you previously practiced. Remember to focus on the exhale, allowing the inhale to happen naturally. With each one, feel your belly snapping back. It will feel like you are pumping your abdomen. After 20 exhales, take a deep inhale and hold the breath for a count of 10. Feel the air circulate throughout your torso, creating space and room for energy to roam. Take your normal exhale, letting all of the air out. This is one complete round. Practice a second round, ending with another long inhale and full exhale. Slowly open your eyes, observing the space you feel in your body and freedom in your energy.

SOLAR PLEXUS VISUALIZATION

Our energetic body is composed of seven chakras, or wheels of energy. The chakra system begins at the base of the pelvis and continues through the body to the crown of the head. The third chakra is the solar plexus, or Manipura chakra, and relates to the energy of Aries. This chakra sits at the bottom of the rib cage and relates to our willpower, how we assert ourselves, and our internal fire. When our third chakra is blocked, we feel disempowered. We are unable to make decisions and follow through with them, and we ultimately give our power away. We can also feel frustrated with ourselves, suffer from low self-esteem, and avoid taking action toward our soul's purpose. When balanced, though, this chakra helps us trust ourselves, empowers us to take action while not wavering in our decisions, and allows us to appreciate other people's strengths.

On the Aries Full Moon, work with the third chakra to bring it balance, strengthen it, and allow it to help align you with your soul's path. The following is a visualization meditation to help align and recharge your third chakra. If possible, try to do this meditation during the day of the Full Moon. You can also do it at night, but the day is best. Stand outside under the light of the Sun with your bare feet planted firmly on the Earth. Close your eyes and tilt your face toward the Sun, feeling its radiance shining down on you. Reach your arms toward the sky, as if to touch the Sun, and feel its light coming down through your arms toward your heart. Pause here for a moment, feeling each fingertip light up with the energy of the Sun. Slowly lower your hands to your solar plexus right below your rib cage, with your fingertips covering the space between your ribs. Take a deep inhale into this area, seeing it fill with yellow, golden light. Take 5 deep breaths like this, seeing an expanding ball of light at the base of your rib cage. Notice any tightness here and allow it to relax. Also, notice any feelings or visions that arise while breathing into this area. What is this area holding? Does it feel balanced? Does it feel free or restricted? What is it telling you about your willpower?

Release your hands down to your sides, but stay focused on the ball of yellow light at your solar plexus. Begin to see it slowly rotating clockwise. Continue to see the ball of light spinning for the next 5 breaths. When chakras are balanced and free of restriction, they spin evenly and smoothly. As you see your chakra turning, also visualize it radiating outward into the world. See it as your own personal Sun, shining your brilliance. Feel the Sun above you reflected in your solar plexus and feel your power to create the life of your soul's purpose. As you walk through the rest of your day, feel this area leading and empowering you.

ARIES CIRCLE SET-UP

The Full Moon in Aries comes near the end of Libra Season. Both signs enjoy the company of others or time alone. You can choose to practice with friends this Full Moon or with just your own energy. Full Moons are generally beneficial times to gather with other like-minded people and share your experiences. It's a time when we can fully be seen and show up as we are, for others to accept us. If you practice in a group, make sure you are comfortable enough to speak freely about your feelings, your process of release, and your newly formed creations.

ARIES CIRCLE SET-UP

Choose a quiet location to set up your Moon Circle, either inside or outside. Incorporate all the elements, especially the elements of Fire for Aries and Air for Libra. Have plenty of candles or an outside fire. You can incorporate air through auric sprays, feathers to fan the smudge sticks, and even wind chimes to hear the air moving around you. Also, represent Earth and Water to bring in all four elements. You can use crystals to represent the Earth. Carnelian, Fire Quartz, Aragonite, and Howlite are wonderful crystals to align with the energy of Aries. Tourmaline, Lapis Luzuli, Ametrine, Peach Moonstone, and Lepidolite are great crystals to align with Libra's energy. Bring in the Water element through a room diffuser, a vase with flowers in it, or just a simple metal bowl containing water. You can even set up your circle by an ocean, lake or river.

Gather all of your supplies and build your circle. Create an outline with your objects, anchoring the four directions—north, south, east, and west—with either a crystal or candle. If you are creating an altar, set it up in the westerly part of the circle, as this placement facilitates release. To set up an altar, line up crystals of your choice, flowers, and images that inspire you. Since this is a Fire Moon, create a place to burn what you are releasing. Have a metal dish or other container that can safely hold a burning paper. If you choose to burn paper inside, make sure your space is properly ventilated so the smoke has somewhere to go. It is recommended that most burning ceremonies take place outside for safety purposes, which may mean your entire circle takes place outside under the Full Moon.

As you set up the circle, create enough space for everyone to be comfortable. You can anchor the circle with a large crystal or crystal grid in the middle. Once the perimeter is set, cleanse the area with a dried herb bundle or space-clearing spray. Begin cleansing at the easterly point, moving to the south, west, north, then back to the east. Imagine a white light encompassing the circle, protecting it from any outside energies. Light your candles and cleanse yourself with the smudge stick or spray. If you are having guests join you, cleanse their energy before entering the circle. The best way to cleanse the energy is to start from the top of the head and move down to the bottom of the feet. Make sure to cleanse around the body, making a circle with the spray or stick. Do each arm and each leg, not forgetting the bottoms of the feet. Once everyone has entered the circle, pause for a moment to let the energy settle before you begin.

Follow your intuitive guidance when leading a circle. As a guide, begin with each member introducing themselves. Talk about the astrological energy of the day and how it is affecting each one of you. Share and learn from each other about your unique experiences with this Full Moon. Give plenty of space for each person to speak. Follow your conversation with the meditation practice to still the mind. You can then begin the rest of the practices in this book. Do them alone, but share as much, or as little, with the others as you like. Go over questions and continue to learn from each other's perspectives. You can also perform the burning ritual described after the practices. Then pull cards to gain insight and intuition from the Universe on how to move forward knowing that you have cleared away what you no longer want.

Close the circle by giving gratitude to everyone who chose to honor the Full Moon with you. Give thanks to the elements for supporting you and the energy of the Universe for guiding you along the way.

ARIES CARD READING

What energy do I
need to find my
inner passions?

CARD PULLED:

What energy will help
me release anything
that does not align
with my passions?

CARD PULLED:

What energy will help
me find and stay
focused my path?

CARD PULLED:

Reading Cards is a beautiful way to access your intuition and tap into your, and the Universe's, higher wisdom. Anyone can pull cards, as long as you are willing to receive the information they provide. You need no prior experience, or training, just an open and clear mind.

You may use any cards you like for this practice, including but not limited to: Tarot Cards, Animal Medicine Cards, Oracle Cards or any Affirmation Cards. You also can pull cards from a few decks to gain different perspectives. If you are new to card pulling, try to ask only one deck the same question, as asking different decks the same question can become quite confusing. Below are some general guidelines on how to pull cards. Please improvise as needed and above anything else, listen to your intuition.

CLEAR YOUR MIND
A settled, grounded mind is essential for pulling cards. The last thing you want is random thoughts running around when you are trying to receive clear answers from yourself. Practice the breath work and meditation in this workbook to prepare and settle your mind. You may also clear your mind using sound frequencies through singing bowls. These can either be crystal or metal bowls. Play the bowl, or bowls, for about 3-5 minutes to help rid your mind of external noise as you focus on the harmony of the sound.

ARIES CARD READING

PICK YOUR DECK

There are many different decks out there. You can choose as many as you like. Know, though, that they each provide you a different energy or medicine. Tarot Cards are the most popular and should be used carefully. Although very useful, Tarot cards can give the wrong impression if you interpret them harshly. Animal Medicine cards offer different types of messages from the animal realm which can help align with the spirit of nature. These cards give you the medicine you need to apply to your situation or question. Affirmation cards provide you with guidance in the form of words or phrases. When reading these cards, it is best to meditate on what the affirmation means for you. It is also helpful to repeat the affirmation a few times and see how it makes you feel. There are many other cards you can experiment with, like Goddess Cards, Angel Cards, and so on. The important thing to remember with any card is that they each have different angles and sides. There are often a few interpretations of the same card.

SHUFFLE

Shuffle the cards the easiest way for you. Some cards are smaller and can be shuffled like a regular deck of playing cards, while others with take some effort. If all else fails, spread them out on the floor in front of you then regather them. Keep a clear mind while shuffling. You can also repeat " I am open to receiving guidance and intuition." Refrain from asking your questions until the next step.

ARIES CARD QUESTIONS

You are free to ask the deck any questions you need answers to on this Full Moon. The following questions are meant to help you harness the energy of Aries through the cards to clarify some of these energies in your mind. This is a three-part card reading, where you'll ask the deck three questions. Before beginning, spread your freshly shuffled cards in a wide arc in front of you. Use your left middle finger to choose the card, first waving your hand slowly over the cards. You'll feel a magnetic pull, or slight tingle, in your fingertip when you hover over the right card. Chose one card at a time, taking a moment to breathe in between questions. Keep the cards flipped over until you pull all three.

What energy do I need to find my inner passions?

What energy will help me release anything that does not align with my passions

What energy will help me find and stay focused my path?

TAKE THEM IN

Once you have your cards, flip them over. Before looking up their meaning, sit with them for a moment and allow them to speak to you. Intuit your own meaning and interpretation of the card. What is the card trying to tell you? What are you trying to tell yourself? After a few moments with the cards, look up their meaning. Sit with that information, merging it with your intuitive meaning of the cards.

As with everything, enjoy this process. Do not worry if you are doing it right or wrong. Just follow your intuition, and trust the journey. Accept the cards you are dealt and use their energy wisely to help guide you when you need it the most.

ARIES PRACTICES

CREATE A LIFE AROUND WHAT INSPIRES YOU THE MOST

This Aries Full Moon gives us the opportunity to align with our life's purpose. It's a time to understand our personal mission in this world and find purpose in our journey. We all have a calling in this lifetime—a reason our energy showed up in this moment of time. Our energy is on a path of evolution, and it came to this life to find lessons, people, and pathways to growth. When we are aligned with our life's purpose, we feel fulfilled and energized by life. We intuitively know when we are on the right path for our souls. It simply feels right, and we feel we are where we belong.

ARIES PRACTICES

Finding our life's purpose can be a daunting task. Some people will know their mission intuitively. Others will need years of experimentation and open-minded thinking to find their path. Wherever you land on the path to finding your purpose, know that part of this purpose is finding it. Part of walking your life's path is the process of finding it in the first place. Even if it takes you years to figure out your purpose, those years and everything they held are part of finding the mountain you are here to climb. It may feel like your path is winding or takes many turns; there may be times when you can't connect the dots or don't understand why things are unfolding as they are. It's all part of the process of finding yourself.

When you have a firm purpose in this world, you become centered in yourself. It becomes easier to focus your energy and make important life decisions. You know who you are and what you want in life. Your internal compass is finely tuned and you do not spend hours deliberating between choices. It also becomes easier to hold visions for your intentions. Often when we set intentions, we lose them after a few weeks when life distracts us. When we understand and trust our path, holding the vision of our future becomes effortless and grounded in truth. We no longer jump from vision to vision; we hold the one we know will help us align with our life's purpose. We may evolve this vision as we grow, but its core remains the same.

Once you have found your life's calling, you then begin. The act of starting on your path can be harder than finding it in the first place! Aries is the energy of new beginnings. This energy always exists in the world; the Full Moon just amplifies it. You can always tap into the vibrations of Aries to help you take the first steps on your path. First, though, you must find any blocks that prevent you from taking a leap of faith. There are many obstacles, both external and internal, that prevent you from starting on your path. Most of these blocks, though, will be in your own mind. They come in the form of self-doubt, fear of success, fear of failure, and fear of commitment, among others. This Full Moon is an opportunity to release any of your internal blocks preventing you from beginning on the path you know is meant to be yours.

Once you do begin, then comes the journey of continuing on your path. There will always be challenges, but how you deal with these challenges is what makes all the difference. Again, the energy of Aries can give you the stamina and motivation needed to continue on your path. It is not always easy to remain motivated. Burnout is real and can rob you of the joy that comes from being on your soul's path. Even when you do find your purpose, not every day will be easy or without challenge. It's important, though, to always remember why you began. It's important to remember the feeling of first finding your purpose and letting that feeling motivate you to continue. It's also important to take breaks when you need them and find methods of restoring your fire. These methods will change over time, but it's essential to continue to find ways to make your fire burn bright again if it becomes diminished.

The following questions are designed to help you explore your purpose. Really, what you are searching for is how you want to spend your time on this planet. This search is an ongoing exploration and one that could take many Moons. Do not feel you have to answer all of these questions, or that you need to answer them all in one sitting. Take your time with them, and allow the answers to unfold organically. Begin your exploration with these questions. But more importantly, open your mind to the possibility of who you could be.

ARIES PRACTICES

1. Do you have any intuitive guidance on what your purpose is in this world? If the answer is yes, are you ignoring your intuition? If the answer is no, how can you create space to allow your intuition to be heard?

2. Finding your purpose requires knowing what doesn't fit with your ultimate life's mission and releasing it. What are some past visions of yourself that you, or others, may have held that no longer resonate with your true purpose?

ARIES PRACTICES

3. What activities give you energy? Which ones drain you?

ARIES PRACTICES

4. What would your eight-year-old self be doing right now?

_____

_____

_____

_____

_____

_____

_____

_____

_____

_____

_____

_____

_____

5. What are your unique gifts? These are the energies or perspectives you can offer the world that no one else can.

_____

_____

_____

_____

_____

_____

_____

_____

_____

_____

_____

ARIES PRACTICES

6. What do you become completely absorbed in? Meaning, what activities capture your full attention and make it feel like time no longer exists?

_____

_____

_____

_____

_____

_____

_____

_____

_____

_____

7. Do you begin things easily? If yes, can you sustain this motivation? If no, what prevents you from starting something? Furthermore, what motivates you to begin and how can you incorporate that into your life more?

_____

_____

_____

_____

_____

_____

_____

_____

_____

_____

ARIES PRACTICES

8. Recognizing the difference between external and internal blocks is an important part of walking your path. Write down some external blocks you've experienced, like the weather or travel delays. Write down internal blocks you've experienced, like limiting beliefs or self-doubts.

_____

_____

_____

_____

_____

_____

_____

_____

_____

_____

_____

9. What types of adversity help you grow? Every dream has challenges. Our true purpose will bring us challenges that propel our evolution and, in the end, help us along our path.

_____

_____

_____

_____

_____

_____

_____

_____

ARIES PRACTICES

10. Finally, what do you want to be remembered for doing? What is your legacy?

BURNING RITUAL

Complete the practices in this workbook, then feel into everything you want to release this Aries Full Moon. Focus primarily on the answers to the first three questions to understand the energies that block you from releasing your true potential and purpose.

This releasing ritual uses the element of Fire to help you eliminate anything you no longer want to carry. When you feel centered in your power, write down energies you no longer want in your life. These can be emotions you are ready to release, behaviors that are no longer beneficial, or relationships that no longer support you. You can also release your excuses, stories, and the myriad of negative mantras you may tell yourself to remain small or not take up the space you deserve. Write freely, allowing your consciousness to dump on the paper.

When you've finished, close your eyes and hold the piece of paper in front of your face. Inhale into your chest. As you exhale, imagine the energy you want to release leaving your field and landing on the paper. Repeat this breath three times. Reopen your eyes and take the paper to the fire.

Burn the page in a metal dish or another safe container in a properly ventilated room so the smoke, and energy, have a place to escape. You may also burn it in an outside fire. Watch the page go up in flames, turning into ashes, and see your energy transform in front of you. If possible, collect some of the ashes from the burned paper. Place them in the bowl of water with a clear quartz crystal to be further cleansed. This final step is not needed for release but can help enhance the ritual. Let the water sit for twenty-four hours, then throw it in a body of water or down the drain.

BURNING RITUAL

After performing this burning ritual, answer the following questions:

How does it feel to create space in your energy through release?

_____

_____

_____

_____

_____

_____

_____

_____

What mantra can help you keep this space clear and prevent yourself from falling back into old habits?

_____

_____

_____

_____

_____

_____

What mantra can help call in the energy you want to accompany this new space in your energetic field?

_____

_____

_____

_____

_____

_____

_____

LAST QUARTER IN CANCER

Last Quarter Moon occurs when the Moon makes it to the last quarter of the lunar cycle, completing her journey around the Earth back to the Sun. On the Last Quarter Moon, we see a Half Moon in our sky, signifying a 90° separation, or square aspect, between the Sun and the Moon. Squares bring up friction and often crises in our energetic body. They feel tense to us, and we can either choose to resist them or work with the energy presented. If we decide to lean into the Last Quarter's energy and opportunity, we tap into a powerful force of release. The Last Quarter Moon's energy encourages us to surrender to what we cannot control and let go as we make space for new energy. There is often an epiphany at this stage of the lunar cycle, when we realize the person we can become if we can finally release an old pattern, emotion, or attachment.

The Last Quarter journey is not always an easy one; we must be willing to confront places of resistance within ourselves. These are the areas that hold on to energies that are no longer serving our highest visions. We may feel a loss during this time or even some grief for the things we are releasing. Embrace these feelings, knowing they are part of the process of transformation. Also, know that to call in new energies, you must let go of the things that block you or lower your frequency, even if they feel comfortable. Trust the process of your release and embrace the witness consciousness to help you through this time.

The energy of Cancer brings our emotions to the surface of this Moon and our intuition. Cancer reminds us to feel all of our emotions and allow ourselves to be vulnerable. With the Sun still in Libra, expect this to be an emotional day for relationships. Feel into Libra's energy, helping you calm and center yourself before communicating with any of your partners. Do, though, take inspiration from Cancer to freely express your feelings and share your subjective world with those around you.

The Moon in Cancer is very healing. Her energy can help heal broken partnerships and relationships. She can also help heal our relationship with ourselves. Spend some time over the next few days journaling, using the element of Water in cleansing rituals, and opening yourself to your intuition through meditation. Apply what you learn during this time to your partnerships, helping them grow with you.

This Last Quarter Moon is a time to shed your reservations about expressing your true emotions and intuition. The energy of Cancer is very powerful and reminds us that we each hold the power of the divine feminine within us. We can feel our future and see our highest visions once we allow ourselves to feel our emotions. When we suppress or hide our true feelings, we also suppress our intuitive knowing. Give yourself time to feel this last Quarter, then from a grounded place, permit yourself to share those feelings with those around you. Also share your intuition with those around you. Sharing your intuitive information can make you feel vulnerable, but trust yourself and those around you to support you. Your intuition is more valuable than you could ever imagine. Share it with the world.

What are you willing to let go this
Last Quarter Moon to allow yourself to
receive new energy?

AFFIRMATIONS

Think of three people who can be role models of purpose for you. They can be someone in your life or someone you have never met. Name three qualities each of these people possess.

_____

_____

_____

_____

_____

_____

_____

_____

_____

_____

Now write three mantras based on these qualities that you can repeat to yourself every day.

Example: My friend Jackie works hard, confronts adversity, and trusts herself. Mantra: I trust myself to work hard and face adversity with grace.

_____

_____

_____

_____

_____

_____

_____

_____

HAPPY
FULL MOON!

Thank you to everyone who supported and purchased this workbook.

Special Thanks to Rebecca Reitz (rebeccareitz.com, @becca_reitz) for her beautiful artwork on the cover & pages 2, 4, 10, 16, 22, 32.

For a monthly subscription contact hello@spiritdaughter.com or visit www.spiritdaughter.com.

Disclaimer: The exercises and yoga sequences in this book are physical activities that should be performed carefully to avoid injury. You agree to accept all risks and release Spirit Daughter and any guest instructors from any and all liabilities. Please take care and enjoy.

Follow along our journey on IG:
@spiritdaughter

We always love seeing your photos & hearing about your experiences with the workbooks! Tag us to be featured on our community page:
@spiritdaughtercollective